CONFESSIONS OF A COFFEE LOVER

POETICAL CONFESSIONS

ROHINI RAMESH

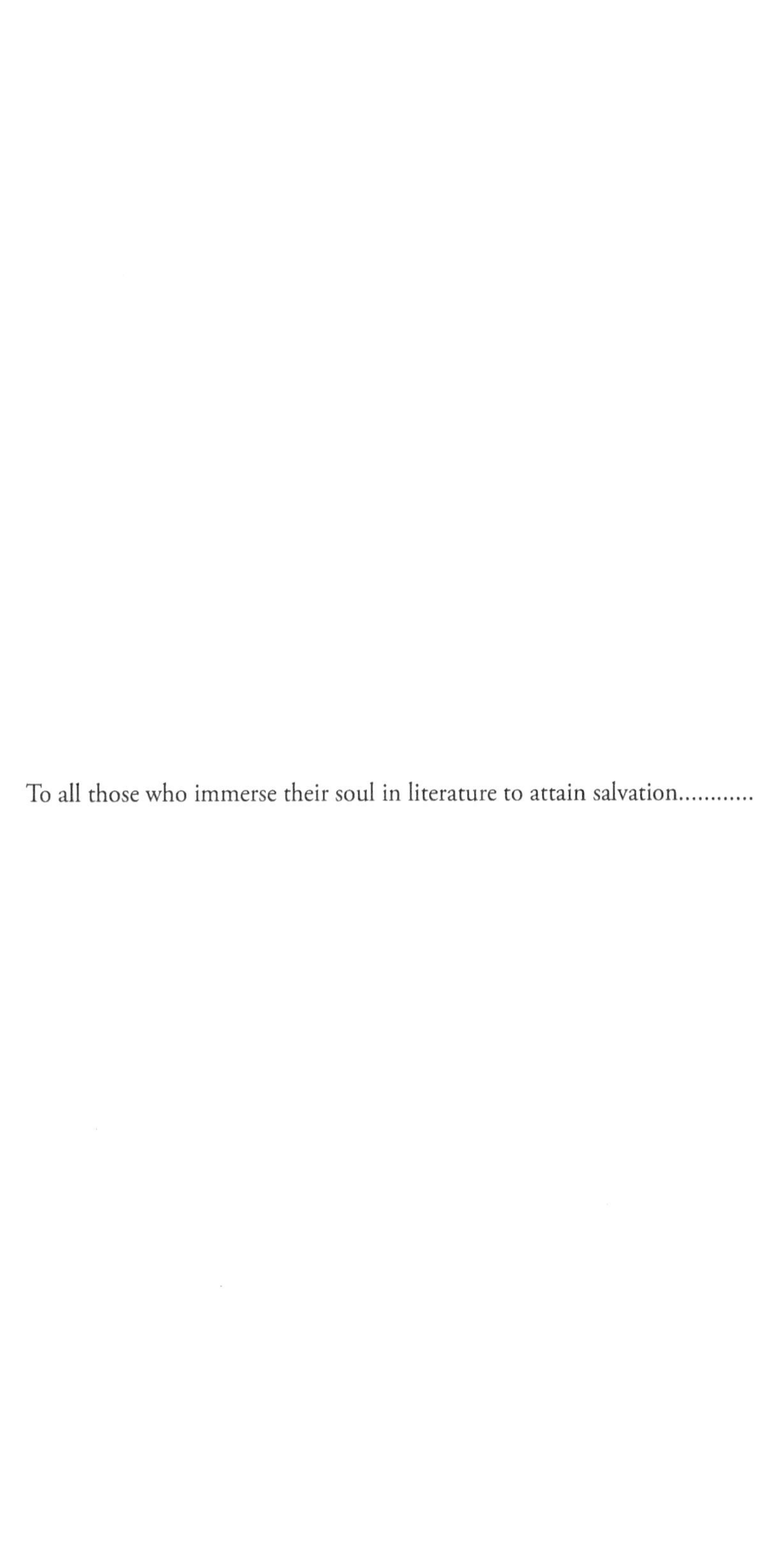

To all those who immerse their soul in literature to attain salvation............

Contents

Contents

Preface

I've been penning poems ever since, I started having mood swings. A lot of things grabbed my attention and they have a serious impact on my psyche. This book is an outlet for all those pent-up emotions, ideas, and thoughts. This work would give the readers an insight into common things with an uncommon perspective. This may also help the readers to look forward to things in a non-conservative look and have rational thoughts.

Foreword

Some people speak. Some people scream. My sister writes.

I've seen my sister write through silences that felt like storms. Not all revolutions begin with

noise — some are born at a desk, with ink, coffee, and an aching heart. "Confessions of a Coffee

Lover" is one such revolution. This book is not just a collection of poems. It is a battlefield of

emotions, where words rise like soldiers — fragile, furious, honest — each poem standing as a

flag she has planted on the soil of her experience.

As her brother, I have stood at the edge of her world, watching as she built this quiet rebellion

word by word. She didn't need a stage or a spotlight. She created her own—with a cup of coffee

by her side, and a heart that refused to stay silent. These poems are her voice in a world that

often tells women to whisper. This book is her stage, and she has stepped onto it not for

applause, but for truth.

So read these pages slowly. By reading these poems, you'll find a woman asking the world hard

questions—and sometimes not waiting for an answer. And if you're willing to really listen, you

might meet parts of yourself too.

She wrote her heart out—and gave it a name. And now, as you hold it in your hands, I hope you carry it gently. Not just because it's hers, but because it might just become yours too.

— Hariprasath

(Brother & the First Reader of Her Unfinished Storm)

Acknowledgements

I would like to acknowledge my guardian angel, my grandparents in heaven, my parents, my sister, and all my family members for everything they have done for me. I extend my heartfelt thanks to my friends, and well-wishers for their continued support and patience. I am grateful to my little brother Hari for helping me in designing the cover page of this work. I wish to earn their favour and trust through my work. I am grateful to everyone who helped me directly or indirectly to bring out this book.

1. Listener

All I crave for is a listener
Who can let me own their ears, sometimes mind too
For a few minutes, or
Maybe for some hours,
Until the eerie thoughts creeping in
Put a stop.
All I need is a listener
Who is ready to put their legs in my show
And understand what I'm going through
Until the pressure climbing up
Stops accumulating.
A conversation would do,
May be at a coffee table
Or even a terrace would do fine!
Sea shores can calm me but
I want to be listened, not the waves!
I tried, cried, and strived
To find a listener and
Just ended up meeting whistle-blowers.

2. Matrimony

First, it makes a lot of people get modified
And later it makes them get commodified!
It makes people lose themselves
To find someone for themselves!
It's just a modern Market
Which sells goods with soul and life!

3. Alterations

4. Marriage

Once, it was said that
Marriages are made in heaven
And everything was supposed to be in even.
And now, I find the real face of marriage,
It's just a custom related to age
All that matters is a man's wage!
Turning the next page
I just found that it's a baggage
Filled with caste, religion, and honor
Not only of the partners
But of the entire family.
What that wonders me
Is the luggage the bride carries..
Gold, Silver, Cash and goods set
And the weightage of the groom
With job, home and asset!
Marriage,
It seems like a business to me
Where people exchange wealth
For the union of two and
This is so blue!

5. Kitchen Sink

I know she is sulking in pain
And all her emotions are getting drowned in the drain!
This might be a refrain
Of all the mothers who are the family's marginalized main!
Whenever there is a chaos
She bends, sometimes even break
But holds the family together !
Wherever there is a wreck
She repairs, sometimes even replace
But never throws anything out!
Whichever is her favourite
She loses it or sacrifices it
But had never complained about it!
Whoever shouts at her,
She smiles, sometimes cries in silence
But never lets her lungs out!
Does these sound good??
She is the silenced swan with a working mouth
Probably, stitched with patriarchy, culture and conventions.
She is the chained maiden,
Married, hopefully to a kitchen sink and not a man.

6. Tissue Paper

7. What If She Does?

You came late at night

After a movie, party, night out

and you wanted her to welcome you with open arms!

Serve you food and make you feel good!

and the other day,

She was late by an hour

For she had works crossing the bar,

You yelled at her

Abused her. Called her names

And you do the same

Not once, twice or thrice

But every time.!

After hurting her with words like a sharp knife

You went out picnics, tours and enjoying life

Where as she was crying all night, Remember she is your wife.!

At times,

You were wailing in pain

And that innocent soul made her soul drain

For you!

But, When she wanted to have a talk

Sorry, you always used to stand and walk

saying you have plans with your clan!

She wasn't a overthinker

You made her one.

She wasn't a impatient fool
It's you who made her lose her cool!
Once, she was flying free like a dove
you were craving for her love
She is yours now,
And you constantly tear her apart and she doesn't know how?
What if she does the same?
Avoiding you, abusing you and stop loving you?
Will it be okay?
Start treating her better
Before she says it's over!

8. Broken Women

Stronger than bricks
They have been made so by some cheap tricks
Of some mean women and men.
Heated and baked in disloyalties
Cheated and faked by trusted communities
That's how they are made!
Drowned in tears
They wiped all their fears.
Hiding themselves in the dark
They started making a mark.
From being shy and tender
To become strong and braver.
Left alone with none to trust
They prevented them from getting rust
Burying the memories of the best times
Worrying about the next times.
Soaked in hurt and sour
They are broken in the crust and core
But filled with rage and courage,
They mature with passing age!
Arrogant, that's how the world perceives them
But they are actually independent.

9. Sunshine

He told her that she was his sunshine
Still he made her whine!
She just lit his world up
but found that he had another when she is not up!
In her absence, she thought, he had only darkness
But he had a moon and millions of star
He took all the light from her
Yet said she was emitting heat!
She gave him light to adorn things
and he learnt to fly with bright wings!
It was then she realized, she just had paper rings
And there is gonna be new beginnings!
She was just that free resource
And he felt bored with the time's course
Now, She was just removed by force
Poor girl,
She was one of his whores.

10. Silence

When the world is looking at things which are violent
I'm here staying silent
Not because I'm ignorant
But, because I am ignored!
I have rage pumping up my spine
And woes filling up my brain
Still I choose to remain quiet
Because I'm too tired to fight!!
Being left alone is not new to me
That's the usual me
Unbothered by others' actions
and giving them no reaction!!
But, this time it hurts
For I've trusted people who doesn't deserve
and kept myself on reserve!
How stupid I've been
To rely on people who are so mean!
I've too much in my mind
But I don't want anybody to find!
I am crying here in vain
And I don't want anyone to know my pain!
That's why decided to be silent!
You know what?? My mouth is at mute
But my mind is there., Screaming louder than

The world could ever hear!

11. Sharp-edged Words

They just pour like rain
Causing a lot of tears and pain
Unexpected and Unbearable
That's how unique they are.
Boneless part rolls and trills
And the resultant words make you grill,
Sometimes comes out of will
And it just makes you mentally ill.
Friend or foe,
If you want to have a war,
Swords are better because they hurt the body
Bitter words are toxic because they kill souls!

12. Wasted Souls

Hey society!
Stop being so judgmental.
Some people get married because they are wild
And definitely they don't need a child!
You start terming them infertile
And make them ail!
Along which you give a huge prescription
So that they can have a child for description!
Stop this!
Some people are mentally incapable of being parents
And they can never stop their rants!
They can never take care of a child
And the child's trauma goes unfiled!
They can neither provide attention nor
stop giving the child tension!
They can neither understand nor
Let the child stand up!
So, next time when you see such people,
Better gift them a pack of condom
So that they can avoid wasting souls in random.

13. Torn Letter

When you just received me
You were brimming with pride
As if you got a royal carriage ride!
You read me a hundred times
Enjoying each and every single line
Knowing that it was love's sign!
Then came new letters
And in a file I was neatly placed
And soon after I was replaced!
I am boring and unworthy
Since you know me already, I begged
Read me one more time and you are not ready!
With time I lost my value
I became torn and old
And to me you are always cold!
I still think of all those times
When you craved for alone nights to read me
And to everywhere you go you sneak me!
Oh with time!
People forget everything!
All I wonder is...
Have I lost importance or
The one who wrote lost importance?

14. Unclean

I am bleeding, yes I'm.
I am undergoing a lot of pain
And I am not crying in vain!
Yes! I am menstruating.
I feel cramps and I can't walk ramps.
And you are telling me don't light the lamps.
Not out of concern... definitely not
At times, I get moody
And I shout at you in phone
Sorry, it's coz of my hormone.
And, you people filled with brains
Tell me... Apologies Instruct me... command me
Stay away from deities!
I pity you!
It's the same Deity which created me
Had made me bleed every month.
Yet, you want me stay away
As If I'm impure..
Oh dear... I'm pure... my heart is pure
It's you and your ideology
Which is sour.
You call me unclean..!
Pardon me! It's your heart which is mean and unclean.

15. 15 Seconds

It takes just fifteen seconds
That makes one to meet dead ends,
Enough to destroy a strong foundation
Which holds any relation!
Fifteen seconds!
That's all it takes
To crush a heart
And break it into parts!
To rip the soul in whole
Out of the body, it takes only fifteen seconds.
To say the meanest words
And to play the cleanest games
All it requires is
Just fifteen seconds!
From five to fifty
All of us, for at least fifteen times
Would have wanted to change some
FIFTEEN SECONDS for the better!

16. Decisions

Every Left and Right we take
Impacts the decision we make.
Some are influenced by situations
Others manipulated by people.,
Some listen to their mind
While others say Never mind.,
Some hear the heart's voice
And others become society's toys.,
Some choose the familiar
But a few wants their life to be peculiar.,
Some make mistakes,
But others might miss a take.,
Some are indeed cool,
Whereas others all fate's fool!
In the end,
What counts is not success
But all that matters is
How happy the journey was!

17. Protection

You love them, help them..
I don't mind because
I care no more for relations
You think I'm a coward?
Not at all...
I've fought the worst times all alone.
Endured the pain for ages unknown.
You should have known
But you didn't.
Today,
You want to protect me...
Sorry, I don't need that!
For you failed when I needed that!
And I know how to give people a cut.!!

18. Sneakers

This thing never goes out of trend
For it has never actually witnessed an end.
They are usually quiet and traceless
And every time they are ruthless
Sorry! I'm not penning about a product
But about a problem
That's been a part of daily life.
When I was ten,
And I never knew these men
From the backseat of a public transport
He just extended his hands like I was his sport
Startled by a strange touch
I just moved forward an inch
And the one sitting near me sensed the inconvenience
And took me to another seat with all the dead silence
That night, I had million rational questions on my mind
But there were no answers, I could find.
From then, this never went out of trend
And I just switched seats like they were nothing I could mend.
Then I was twenty One
When Actually I found I can be the one
Who could clutch and cut the uncontrollable hands
Of the inevitable sneakers!
This time, I was alone

And It happened again and I managed to use a blade
And make him bleed!
All in silence it took place
For, I was scared in first place
About making some noises
And hearing all those judgmental voices.
That satisfaction I had that night
And all I could see was light.
Then I grew a bit older and a bit bolder
And in five more years
I dared to stand up against all my fears!
I clutched the collar of another perpetrator!
And I gave a loud voice
For I don't want any more kids to be their toys.

19. Wounds That Never Heal

We all have a scar

Which still oozes out

And this time the pain is more

Does the wound remain unhealed, I doubt!

The searing pain and souring memories

All the cries that went in vain

Still makes me nauseous

And reminds me to be cautious!

For them, It might not be a big deal

But I still fail to heal!

Till date, I am trying to find a medicine

To cure someone else's sin!

SIN

That ruptured my innocence

And make my heart fuming with vengeance!

There are wounds which no doctors can cure

Because I know they're invisible to others' eyes for sure.

20. Truth

It was dark, dreamy and quiet,
And I was immersed in my own thoughts!
Everything is just a mess
And I couldn't even guess!!
Sometimes we learn the TRUTH in the hardest way,
Accepting it becomes a dismay!
Some people, after knowing the truth
Remain quiet with a sulky face
While others fight in a hulky pace!
Truth is not always sweet
And sometimes it's something not to greet!
To some Truth is everything they seek!
To some, Truth is everything they speak!
But for me,
Truth is just a word
With no stable meaning!

21. Heads

They say, responsibility comes with position
But I feel, arrogance is the compliment.
Just because you're the head
Doesn't mean we are the tail!
We might be your brain
Which strengthens you!
Or might be the train
Which transports you
To the next level!
You might be old
But that's never a reason to be cold!
You've to obey elders, that's what I've been told,
And that's how we were ruled..
Not for once, but for ever!
Men make themselves the head,
Once they are wed!
And a woman just becomes someone for the bed,
and prepares the bread.

22. Spoilers

There are spoilers in every family
Some are always numb
Others are so dumb!
Some create issues
Others make us buy tissues!
Some are always crying
Others are probably trying!
Some are loud,
Others are proud!!
It's always a spoiler
Who just ruins every happy time!
With an unwanted smile or sly comment
Which they actually know has the power to torment!!

23. Barking Dogs

Barking Dogs

Every time I hear it,

It's loud and annoying!

Sometimes it's for food..

Sometimes it's the only mood!

Always rude,

And not once for the good!

Sometimes in front of a stranger...

Just to assert its presence!

My aversion is at its peak

But I could never speak!

For I know it is useless

To speak with something senseless!

It has always been persistent in my mind

And the answer, I could never find

Why do the hypocrites,

Shouts and Scowls every time

To assert that they lead the family?

24. The Valley

It was loud, messy and cinematic
But the serenity sustained
For they were the noise made by
Happy screams of kids,
Couples doing crazy reels and
Families enjoying their vacation.
Ziplines taking people from one end to another
Boats carrying tourists in the crystal clear lakes!
It was indeed a happy view!
Somewhere amidst this,
Came a chaos
Bullet noise silenced the screaming kids
Violence silenced the happy families!
Shocked, Panicked, and struck by terror
Everyone figured out
The upcoming horror
Newly wed became a widow.,
The captain became a corpse.
The greenest of valleys became red and
Innocents lay there injured and dead!
That's how a serene tourist spot
Became a terrorist lot.

25. Victory

It was a wait of eighteen years
To be precise, a penance
But in the end it turned out to be a menace.
The streets of the city,
Were overflowing with happy faces
Even kids were making cheerful noises
For the King, his team and the Cup
Winning the cup is a long story
But something else made into history!
Celebrations became wild and clumsy
That the screams for help became mild and lousy,
Under the noise of boos and hooos
People were dying trampled by some shoes
Planned to be a celebration which is rapid but
Destined to be a stampede.

26. We Are Here, Not Them

The headlines in block letters
Mentioned the sexual assault of a kid!
All breaking news were breaking
Details of the assault!
HOW, WHEN, WHO, WHERE and WHAT?
The issue was burning like
Old clothes burnt with petrol
And the discussions about it
Went out of control!
East or West
Every citizen found this talk the best!
And I was scrolling through social media
Found a video of an influencer
Interviewing someone of the third gender!
He asked her about this issue
And I was about to scroll
Then I heard this sentence from her
"Come to us if it urges you, fools, don't prey on the innocent souls."
For a second, I got numb!
What a bold statement with a casual tone,
Which would slap the perpetrators
And make them groan.

27. Shattered Dreams

Along with the fumes and flames
Is burning thousands of dreams
Dream of
Starting a new life
Celebrating birthday with wife
Breaking all the barrier
And building a new career!
Along with broken wings
Is dying the hope,
The Hope of
A Father waiting for his son, who promised to retire and spend some more
time with him;
And families trying to finding their dear ones ALIVE!
Their suitcases were safe! I Heard
Can't it be the opposite?
The people safe and luggages burnt!
Along with the plates of lunch remains,
Remains my heart, reminding all the white coat warriors
Who were hoping to serve the needy
But all it was found was their dead body!
Sorry, remains of their dead body.
Legs, hands, heads scattered all around.
One survived, A Miracle, Everyone posted!
Can't there be one more, or ten more

I prayed
But the NEWS broke, Everyone else is no more.
I pray, at least this prayer be answered
Not of me but of the nation!
Let them have a painless afterlife, a peaceful one
Unlike the air crash, which ruined everything they were.

28. The Girl Who Conspired

It was a perfect day
And everyone was really gay,
The two young souls United into one
And the boy smiled like he had won!
There were a lot of reels taken
Matching outfits, crazy moves and celebrating love
And he thought it was all real!
They planned their dream trip,
And she planned something else,
Amidst the misty mountains
She murdered the man she married
And became the girl who murdered.
It wasn't a marriage out of love
Screamed everyone
Some said it's for money,
Some said it's for another boy!
Others said, oh god she is such a shame
Spoiling the family name!
The truth is yet buried within her
And the pain of betrayal still prevails in the corpse
Of the man, Who loved the wrong girl!

29. Silences

One day,
There was a meaningless conversation and
She chose to stay silent
For she knew there was nothing she could do about that!
The other day,
It was a meaningful argument but
It's not about her and she chose to stay quiet!
Another day,
It was an outrageous argument
Partially associated with her,
And she peeped out but kept her lips sealed.
Few weeks ago,
There was a loud argument
Entirely about her,
She came out and went back without a word!
Last week,
There was a sensitive argument
About her and everything around her,
But she didn't give a shit and kept her mouth shut.
Today,
There was a triggering argument
Which triggers the trauma of abuse, for her dear one...
And she knows she was the only witness for the victim!
And this time she chose

Silence again!

30. Day and Night

Light is there everywhere at last

Still, I couldn't see what I lost!

Here and there, I wander without peace

In search of finding the missing piece!

Is that shiny? I don't know!

Was then rainy? You won't know!

It just melted just like snow

And I was crying, Oh NO!

Oh my God! The light is gone

And Now I am Night's pawn

I have to wait till the dawn

and I should mend what is torn!

With every second of darkness

I try to forget what was done

But by that I just lose my happiness

I strive to have gay and fun

But all I have is blinded eye

And I am here with just a sigh!

Without knowing what I lost.

About The Poet

Rohini Ramesh

Rohini is a young and talented charm of twenty-five and started her career as an Assistant Professor of Literature. She is always easy to watch but hard to catch. She always stood in the spotlight from early childhood and enjoyed being there. With every passing year, she moved a bit closer to her dreams. She never minds falling down, for every time she gets up stronger. Her failures made her invincible. She is a Bibliophile who loves fantasizing. When life was so unfair to her, she welcomed it with open arms. She vents all her pains and disappointments by penning poems. She has been blessed with a beautiful and happy family, making her an independent and strong person. She is never scared of voicing those ideals and ideas that have been kept concealed. After her first work, *Bloom,* this second book again tries to curb the stigma of adhering to norms, which is prevalent in society.